SPACE GUIDES

DISCOVERING THE SOLAR SYSTEM

PETER GREGO

Copyright © 2007 QEB Publishing

First published in the United States by
QEB Publishing, Inc.
23062 La Cadena Drive
Laguna Hills, CA 92653

This edition published by
Teacher Created Resources, Inc.
6421 Industry Way
Westminster, CA 92683

www.teachercreated.com

All rights reserved. No part of this publication may be reproduced, stored in a retrieval
system, or transmitted in any form or by any means, electronic, mechanical, photocopying,
recording, or otherwise, without the prior permission of the publisher, nor be otherwise
circulated in any form of binding or cover other than that in which it is published and
without a similar condition being imposed on the subsequent purchaser.

Library of Congress Control Number: 2007001016

ISBN 978 1 4206 8267 0

Written by Peter Grego
Produced by Calcium
Editor Sarah Eason
Illustrations by Geoff Ward
Picture Researcher Maria Joannou

Publisher Steve Evans
Creative Director Zeta Davies
Senior Editor Hannah Ray

Printed and bound in China

Picture credits
Key: T = top, B = bottom, C = center, L = left, R = right, FC = front cover, BC = back cover

Corbis/Eugen/Zefa 9, /NASA 8–9, /Robert Weight/Ecoscene 11T; **CTIO**/NOAO/AURA/NSF 7B;
Getty Images/Amana 14B, /Iconica 11B, /Photodisc FCT, FCC, 8, 12, 18, 21T, 27B; **NASA** 1–5,
10, 13B, 17T, 17B, 19T, 19B, 21B, 22, 25T, 25B, 28, BC, /ESA/M. Robberto and the Hubble Space
Telescope Orion Treasury Project Team 6, /The Hubble Heritage Team (STScI/AURA) 24, /JPL 13T, 14T,
15, /JPL-Caltech 7T ; **Peter Grego** 23B; **Science Photo Library** 24, /Harvard College Observatory
29, /Mark Garlick 20, FCB, /NASA 22–23, /NASA/ESA/STSCI/Erich Karkoschka/University of Arizona
26, /Sheila Terry 27T, /Detlev Van Ravenswaay 28–29; **Wikipedia Commons Public Domain** 5.

Web site information is correct at time of going to press. However, the publishers cannot
accept liability for any information or links found on third-party Web sites.

Words in **bold** can be found in the Glossary on pages 30–31.

Contents

Our cosmic backyard

Our **planet**, Earth, is one of eight planets that make up an area of **space** we call our **solar system**. Inside the solar system are our **sun** and **moon**, and the eight planets: Mars, Venus, Mercury, Earth, Jupiter, Saturn, Uranus, and Neptune. The solar system also includes the moons that orbit around Uranus and Neptune, and many comets and **asteroids**.

Mercury

The four inner planets

The four planets nearest the sun are Mercury, Venus, Earth, and Mars. These are called the four "inner planets." Each has a solid surface and, except Mercury, is surrounded by an **atmosphere**. Only Earth's atmosphere is suitable for us to breathe.

The four outer planets

The four "outer planets" are Jupiter, Saturn, Uranus, and Neptune. These are giant balls of mainly **hydrogen** and **helium** gas and are the planets farthest from the sun.

sun

Mars

4

The four inner planets of ⇧ our solar system: Mercury, Venus, Earth, and Mars.

The dwarf planets

As well as the eight major planets, a few smaller solid balls orbit the sun. These are called "**dwarf planets**." They include the largest asteroid, Ceres, and the frozen worlds of Pluto and Eris.

Biography

Johannes Kepler (1571–1630) and his planetary laws

Four hundred years ago, the German astronomer **Johannes Kepler figured out that all planets in the solar system travel around, or orbit, the sun in an oval-shaped path called an "ellipse." The nearer a planet moves toward the sun, the faster it travels. As the planet moves away from the sun, it slows down. This rule is the same for all orbiting objects —a moon orbiting a planet or a comet orbiting the sun.**

⇐ Johannes Kepler.

Venus

Comets

Comets are mountain-sized, dirty snowballs. They are mainly found in the far reaches of space, at great distances from the sun. Whenever their orbit takes them close to the sun, they heat up and throw off clouds of dust and **gas**.

Earth

Formation of the solar system

Around 4.6 billion years ago, scientists believe that something amazing happened in our **galaxy**, the Milky Way. A star exploded, sending a ripple through a large cloud of nearby dust and gas. The ripple squashed the cloud together, making it thicker in parts.

Gravity pulled on the thicker areas, which collapsed in on themselves. As the cloud collapsed, it began to spin faster and faster. This made it become flatter, thinner,and cooler toward the edges, and hotter at its center. Clumps of material in the cloud then began to stick together. As these areas became larger, gravity caused them to attract other clumps of material. The clumps of material became bigger and bigger, and eventually grew into the planets, moons, asteroids, and comets that make up our solar system.

⬆ The sun was born inside a big cloud of gas and dust, called a nebula.

Birth of the sun

The temperature at the center of the collapsing Milky Way gas cloud became so high that it caused a huge reaction, called a **nuclear reaction**. This created the sun.

The incredible heat and energy made by the newborn sun cleared away the gases and ice in the inner part of the solar system. In this gas- and ice-free area are the four solid inner planets. Gas and ice remained in the outer system, which is where the four outer planets (made of gas) are found. The very edge of the solar system is still freezing and here millions of icy comets exist.

⇧ The young sun was surrounded by clouds of dust and gas, which clumped together to create the planets.

This collection of odd looking objects was found in the Carina ⇧ Nebula (within the Milky Way) by a very powerful **telescope** called the Hubble Space Telescope. Each one is thought to be a very young solar system in the making.

Our sun, the nearest star

hurricane

The sun is a star that shines in the same way as any other star—by changing its hydrogen gas to helium gas, which makes light and heat. The sun is an enormous ball made up of mainly hydrogen gas, which is found throughout the **universe**. The sun is incredibly hot—in fact, the **pressure** and heat at the center of the sun is a hundred thousand times hotter than your oven!

All weather on ⇧ Earth is driven by the sun's heat.

⇦ The sun is a giant, glowing ball of gas.

All plant and animal life on Earth depends upon energy from the sun.

Slowly dying

The sun provides Earth with heat and light, which drives our planet's weather and allows life to exist. If the sun were somehow switched off, our planet would become a frozen ball upon which only the simplest life forms could survive.

During the last 4.6 billion years, the sun has been slowly using up its hydrogen gas, which fuels its heat. The sun is now about halfway through its life. Eventually, in the distant future, it will use up all of its fuel and die.

!

Amazing

Burning up energy

Every second, the sun loses four million tons of its weight as it burns up the gas at its center. Despite this, the sun will carry on shining for several billion more years.

Solar spectacles

Astronomers use special telescopes to look at a very hot area above the sun's surface. Here, they can see gigantic flames of hot gases, called **solar** flares and prominences. Sunspots can also be seen on the sun's surface. These are dark spots that are actually very hot and bright, but seem dark because the rest of the sun's surface is even hotter and brighter. Sunspots are caused when hot gases flow around **magnetic fields** on the sun's surface, leaving a slightly cooler, darker-looking central area.

Warning!

Never look directly at the sun with your eyes, and never use binoculars or a telescope to view it. Raw sunlight can damage your eyes and could even make you blind. Astronomers study the sun safely using special telescopes and equipment.

A total **eclipse** of the sun. ⇧

These bright blobs in the sky are called "sundogs." They are caused when sunlight is bent by ice crystals high in the atmosphere, producing a bright spot in the sky on either side of the sun.

Total sunblock!

Sometimes the moon moves between Earth and the sun. This blocks the sun's light and causes a solar eclipse. Most eclipses are just partial (they do not cover the sun completely). Occasionally, the moon completely covers the sun for a few minutes, causing a total eclipse. During a total eclipse, the sky goes dark, bright stars and planets are clear, and the edge of the sun can still be seen around the dark moon.

Light fantastic

Aurorae are fantastic, multicolored lightshows that appear in Earth's atmosphere. They are caused by winds of energy that blow from the sun. Aurorae are best seen from **polar areas** because the winds from the sun travel along the magnetic fields above Earth's **poles** and cause gases high in the atmosphere to glow. Large aurorae can sometimes be seen from as far south as Florida!

This bright green aurora was seen in the skies above western Iceland.

Mercury

Mercury is the planet closest to the sun. It orbits the sun incredibly quickly, making four complete journeys around it every year. As Mercury is so close to the sun, it never moves far from its glare. It moves so quickly that it can only be seen from Earth six times a year, for two weeks at a time. During these times, it is only visible before sunrise or after sunset.

Smallest planet

Mercury is the smallest of all the planets. It has a very thin atmosphere and has no weather at all. With no atmosphere to spread the heat around the planet, there is a huge difference in temperature between its day and night sides. Its sun-facing day side becomes as hot as an oven at its highest setting, while its night side plunges to around twice as cold as the coldest temperature ever recorded on Earth.

Mercury, ⇨ photographed by the Mariner 10 space **probe**.

Caloris crater

⇧ A close-up of Mercury's surface, showing the Caloris **crater** near the shadow at the left.

Enormous crater

Packed with craters, Mercury's rocky surface looks a lot like the moon. The craters were caused by asteroid impacts—city-sized chunks of rock that smashed into the planet's surface. Most of Mercury's craters were made many billions of years ago, shortly after the solar system formed. The planet's biggest crater is a giant scar that was caused by an asteroid. It is called Caloris and the whole of Kansas could fit inside it!

⇩ When it moves directly between the sun and Earth, Mercury is seen as a tiny black dot. This picture shows its path across the sun during the course of the evening of November 8, 2006.

00:00
23:15
22:15
21:15
20:15
19:15

Amazing

Rare sightings

On rare occasions, Mercury moves directly between the sun and Earth, when it can be seen through a telescope for just four hours as a **black** silhouette. **The next time Mercury can be seen in this way will be on May 9, 2016.**

Venus

Venus is the second planet from the sun and is nearly as big as Earth. The Romans named Venus after their goddess of love because it is such a bright and beautiful planet. In fact, it is so bright that it is easy to see in the sky and has even been mistaken for a UFO!

Seeing with radar

Venus is covered with a very cloudy atmosphere. This reflects a lot of sunlight back into space and is what makes the planet so bright. Although the planet's clouds always hide its surface from view, scientists have been able to see below them with space-probe **radars**.

A view of Venus through a telescope.

Venus

Venus and the moon can be seen shining brightly in the evening sky.

Under pressure

If an astronaut stepped onto Venus' surface, he or she would be fried and squashed in just a second!

Probing for information

Several probes have landed on Venus and taken pictures. The planet's surface is blisteringly hot and the pressure of its atmosphere is enormous—equal to the water pressure 3,280 ft. (1,000 m) below sea level! As a result, the probes did not survive for long.

Mountainous landscape

Most of Venus is covered by huge, rolling plains. From these rise a few large **continent**-sized regions, topped with enormous mountain ranges. Venus's highest mountain, Maxwell Montes, is more than 1.8 mi. (3 km) taller than Mount Everest, Earth's highest peak. The planet's largest continent is called Aphrodite Terra and is about the same size as Africa. Any asteroid craters that might have existed on Venus have been worn away by its atmosphere and volcanic eruptions in the past. Venus may still have active volcanoes today.

⇦ Beneath its clouds, Venus has a wonderful landscape of rolling plains, volcanoes, and mountains.

Earth and moon

Planet Earth is the largest of the four inner planets. Along with its **satellite**, the moon, it orbits the sun once a year. The surface of Earth is called the crust and is a thin layer of rock. It includes the continents and the ocean floor. Beneath Earth's surface, it is so hot that solid rock melts into a flowing liquid called **magma**. Magma continually churns beneath Earth's surface and pushes on the solid crust above it.

Moving plates

Earth's crust is a patchwork of large **plates**, which slowly move against each other. When the plates collide with each other, they crumple. This pushes Earth's surface upward to create a mountain range, such as the Himalayas. Where thin ocean crust is forced beneath thicker continental crust, the rocks melt deep inside the hot magma. This melted rock rises like a bubble into the crust above. Volcanoes occur where it breaks through Earth's surface.

Earth seems to be a giant jigsaw when its plates are drawn on a map.

The beautiful, blue planet Earth, seen from space.

Key Concept

Water world

Earth is virtually covered with water—only a quarter of the surface is dry land. To date, it is the only place in the universe where we can be certain life exists.

The moon

The moon is almost as wide as the USA. It orbits Earth once a month. No wind ever blows there, no clouds ever appear in its skies, and no water ever quenches its dry surface. Life never developed on the moon. Some parts of the moon's surface are covered with asteroid craters. There are also many large plains of dark solidified **lava,** known as "seas."

Earth's moon is a lifeless place, covered in asteroid craters.

Mars

Mars is just over half the size of Earth and is the fourth planet from the sun. It takes nearly two years to orbit the sun. Every few years, Mars appears particularly bright for a month or two in the midnight sky, when it is at its closest point to Earth. Believing the planet looked like a drop of blood, the Romans named it Mars after their god of war. Its red color is due to the rust in its **iron**-rich soil.

Mars, viewed by the Mars Global Surveyor.

Mariner Valley

Amazing

Martians!

Astronomers in the 19th and early 20th centuries imagined they had seen a network of straight lines on Mars. Some claimed they might be canals built by intelligent Martians!

Cold, dusty planet

Mars is very cold. It has just a thin atmosphere in which we would not be able to breathe. However, of all the planets in the solar system, Mars is the most similar to Earth. A day on Mars is just a little longer than our own day. The planet also has its own seasons.

Rocky deserts and dust **dunes** spread across Mars, and its poles are covered with ice caps. Mars has **canyons**, such as the Mariner Valley. It also has **gullies**, which show that large amounts of water may once have flowed across its surface when the planet was a lot warmer and wetter than it is today.

⇧ Mount Olympus is a giant extinct volcano that towers above the plains of Mars.

Life on Mars?

It is possible that **primitive** life may have existed on Mars a long time ago. In August 1996, **NASA** claimed it had discovered traces of **fossil bacteria** in a **meteorite** from Mars. There may even be life on Mars today, hidden in its red soil.

⇦ NASA has landed several probes on the surface of Mars, including two robotic, wheeled rovers called Spirit (left) and Opportunity. These two probes discovered that certain rocks and minerals on the planet had formed in water, proving that there was once water on Mars.

Asteroids and dwarf planets

In the 18th century, astronomers discovered a gap in space between Mars and Jupiter. Believing a mysterious planet existed there, they formed a group to search for it. The group was called the "Celestial Police." On January 1, 1800, astronomer Giuseppe Piazzi spotted a faint object slowly orbiting the sun between Mars and Jupiter. It was so small that it simply looked like a point of light, so it was said to be a "**minor planet**" or asteroid. It was later named Ceres.

⬇ As wide as Texas, Ceres is the biggest object in the asteroid belt.

Minor planets

Ceres turned out to be just one of thousands of minor planets orbiting the sun in what we now call the **asteroid belt**, between Mars and Jupiter. Over 30,000 minor planets have been found to date.

Asteroid zone

Asteroids are chunks of rock that formed during the early days of the solar system. Groups of asteroids orbit in front of and behind Jupiter. An asteroid zone also lies farther out between Jupiter and Neptune.

⇧ Large chunks of rock, called meteors, sometimes blaze through our skies and hit Earth's surface, causing craters.

Smashing rocks

Small asteroid chips sometimes land on Earth. They are called meteorites. Sometimes very large chunks of asteroid head our way and blast out craters in Earth's crust. 65 million years ago, an asteroid impact is thought to have wiped out the dinosaurs.

asteroid

The first dwarf planets

At 621 mi. (1,000 km) wide, Ceres is the largest object in the Asteroid Belt. In 2006, Ceres was upgraded from an ordinary asteroid to a dwarf planet. At the same meeting, it was decided to downgrade Pluto from a regular planet (something it had been considered to be since its discovery in 1930) to a dwarf planet. Measuring just 1,485 mi. (2,390 km) across, Pluto was thought to be too small to be a major planet. Another dwarf planet named Eris, slightly larger than Pluto, was discovered in 2003.

⇧ The asteroid Eros is a strangely shaped chunk of rock that is about as big as the island of Manhattan, in New York.

21

Jupiter

Jupiter is the solar system's biggest planet. It is so large that more than a thousand Earths could fit inside it! It is made up mainly of hydrogen and helium gas.

Ball of gas

Jupiter spins on its **axis** once every ten hours—so fast that it bulges out at its center. Its cloudy atmosphere has light- and dark-colored streaks, amazing cloud patterns, and spots. In Jupiter's atmosphere, a storm rages that is larger than Earth! It is called the Great Red Spot and may have swirled around Jupiter's atmosphere for more than 350 years. As Jupiter is a ball of gas, it does not have a solid surface that a space probe could land on. At the planet's center, there may be a core of **molten rock** bigger than Earth.

Jupiter's moons

Jupiter has more than 60 moons. The two largest moons, Ganymede and Callisto, are bigger than the planet Mercury. Io is bigger than our own moon and is covered in active volcanoes. Europa is a little smaller. Scientists think that beneath its icy surface, there may be an ocean of warm, salty water in which primitive sea life has developed.

Europa

Ganymede

Callisto

Io

Viewing Jupiter and its moons

Use a good astronomy **magazine to find the position of Jupiter in the night sky. Then, look at the planet through binoculars. You will probably see a small, bright oval with several dimmer points of light near to it. If you do a drawing that shows the position of these points of light, and do the same again the following night, you will find that they have moved. These are Jupiter's moons.**

Great Red Spot

 Jupiter's Great Red Spot can be seen on its surface.

 Jupiter and its four big moons, Ganymede, Callisto, Io, and Europa.

Saturn

Saturn is the solar system's second-biggest planet. A ball of mainly hydrogen and helium gas, like Jupiter, it bulges outward at its center because it spins so quickly on its axis. It is the least **dense** of all the planets—if it was shrunk to the size of your fist, it would weigh less than a snowball!

Windy planet

Saturn's atmosphere has a few streaky clouds, but it is much calmer than stormy Jupiter. The planet has very high winds, which can be five times faster than the strongest hurricanes on Earth!

⬆ Saturn is famous for its beautiful **rings** of rock and ice.

Saturn's system of rings is one of the solar system's most beautiful sights. This close-up view by the Cassini probe shows that the rings are made up of hundreds of narrow bands.

Rings of rock and ice

From a distance, Saturn's rings look like solid, flattened hoops. They block out the light from the sun to cast dark shadows onto the planet below. The rings are made up of millions of small chunks of rock and ice. Viewed from Earth over the years, the rings appear to open up, close, and open up once more. This is caused by the changing tilt of Saturn as it orbits the sun.

Saturn's moons

Around 60 large moons orbit Saturn. One of them, Titan, is a true giant. Bigger than the planet Mercury, Titan is the only satellite in the solar system that has its own atmosphere. Titan has an icy landscape of hills and volcanoes. It may also have rivers and lakes made up of a **chemical** called methane.

Titan, Saturn's biggest moon. Titan has a yellow surface made of nitrogen and **methane gas**. The yellow surface is hidden behind a veil of blue-green cloud.

Uranus and Neptune

This photograph of Uranus, taken by the Hubble Space Telescope, shows the planet's clouds, delicate rings, and some of its small moons.

moons

Of the eight planets in our solar system, Uranus and Neptune are farthest from the sun. Uranus takes more than a human lifetime to orbit the sun. It is green-blue in color and four times wider than Earth. It was the first planet to be discovered using a telescope. Until then, only Mercury, Venus, Mars, Jupiter, and Saturn were known (the only planets visible to the naked eye). Uranus has many icy satellites, the biggest of which is Titania.

Mysterious planet

During the early 19th century, astronomers discovered that Uranus took an unusual path around the sun. This could only be caused by another unknown planet, farther out in space, tugging on it and so changing its orbit. In 1846, this mysterious planet was seen for the first time and named Neptune,

William Herschel (1738–1822) discovers Uranus

On March 13, 1781, amateur astronomer William Herschel spotted a small circular object that didn't look like a star or comet. It was a mysterious new planet that lay far beyond Saturn. Saturn is the Roman name for the Greek god Cronus. The new planet was named Uranus, in honor of Cronus's father.

William Herschel. The chart he is holding shows his discovery of Uranus.

Neptune

Neptune is the most distant planet in our solar system. Its orbit takes it 30 times farther from the sun than Earth's. On May 29, 2011 Neptune will have made just one circuit around the sun since its discovery in 1846.

Even though Neptune is in distant, freezing space, a lot of activity takes place there. Storms often well up in the planet's cloud belts, blown by the strongest winds in the solar system.

Neptune's biggest moon, Triton, is a frozen world with active, icy volcanoes that spurt out nitrogen gas.

This picture of Neptune was taken by the Voyager 2 space probe in 1987.

Pluto, Eris, and the Kuiper Belt

When tiny, distant Pluto was discovered in 1930, it was initially declared the solar system's ninth planet. Pluto's orbit takes it 50 times farther than Earth from the sun and takes almost 250 years to complete! Pluto is a little smaller than the moon and is one of the few large objects in the solar system still to be seen by a space probe. It has a big satellite called Charon, which is more than half its size. It also has two tiny moons called Nix and Hydra. Even farther from the sun than Pluto is the Oort Cloud, an area of space filled with comets.

The Kuiper Belt

Hundreds of big asteroids exist beyond Neptune in a zone called the Kuiper Belt. In 2003, a Kuiper Belt object slightly bigger than Pluto was discovered and named Eris. Astronomers recently decided that both Pluto and Eris should be classified as dwarf planets, because they are not big enough to be major planets. Our solar system now has just eight planets.

Eris

sun

Eris is so far away that the sun looks like a bright star in its skies.

A space probe took this photograph of Halley's Comet and its stunning tail of dust and rock. The comet's surface is icy and covered in craters. ▷

Comets

Comets are mountains of ice, dust, and rock, which formed in the deep, frozen areas of the outer solar system. A number of comets travel regularly to the inner solar system. The most famous of these is Halley's Comet, which approaches the sun every 76 years. Many billions of comets may exist in the Oort Cloud.

⇧ Pluto's moon, Charon.

⇦ Dwarf planet, Pluto.

Comet tails

When a comet approaches the sun, its icy surface heats up and gives off gases. As the ice melts, bits of dust and rock that were trapped in it are freed. They float into space and trail behind the comet, creating an amazing tail.

Key Concept

Glossary

asteroid   a lump of rock in space

asteroid belt   a band of space between Mars and Jupiter in which thousands of large asteroids are found

astronomer   someone who studies objects in space

astronomy   the scientific study of objects in space

atmosphere   a mixture of gases found around a star or a planet

aurorae   glowing colors in the night sky made when energy from the sun causes gases in the atmosphere to light up

axis   an imaginary line between a planet's north and south poles. Planets spin on their axis

canal   an artificial waterway

canyon   a steep-sided valley

chemical   a substance that is created when atoms change

continent   a large landmass. Earth has five continents.

crater   a circular, bowl-shaped hole in a planet's surface. Craters are blasted out by the impact of an asteroid or the explosion of a volcano.

dense   something that is very heavy compared with its volume

dune   a wind-blown pile of sand

dwarf planet   an object orbiting the sun with enough gravity to be a rounded shape, but too small to be considered a proper planet

eclipse (solar)   when the moon moves between the sun and Earth and it covers the sun's light so that only the edge of the sun can be seen

fossil bacteria   the impression in rock of something that lived long ago

galaxy   a collection of millions, hundreds of millions, or billions of stars, all held together by gravity

gas   a chemical that is not liquid or solid

gravity   a force that acts throughout the universe. Earth's gravity holds you to its surface, and the sun's gravity holds Earth in its orbit. The bigger and more massive the object, the more gravity it has.

gullies   small water-cut valleys

helium   a very lightweight gas

hydrogen   a very light and colorless gas

iron   a metal

lava   hot, molten rock that bubbles up from below a planet's surface (usually through a volcano)

magma molten rock beneath a planet's crust

magnetic fields areas of magnetic energy

meteorite a small rock that has fallen from space onto Earth

methane gas a smelly gas

minor planet an asteroid

molten rock rock so hot that it is melted and runny

moon the moon is Earth's only natural satellite

NASA National Aeronautics and Space Administration, the United States' national space agency

nuclear reaction a burst of energy caused by atoms hitting each other at high speeds

planet a large, round object that orbits a star. The sun has eight major planets—Mercury, Venus, Earth, Mars, Jupiter, Saturn, Uranus, and Neptune.

plate a large portion of Earth's crust floating on the magma

polar areas the regions around a planet's poles

poles points at opposite ends of a planet

pressure the amount of force applied by one substance on another

primitive very simple and undeveloped

probe an automated spacecraft which gathers scientific information

radar a sensing system that uses radio waves to detect physical objects

rings large, flat circular hoops made up of dust, rubble, and/ or ice chunks. Rings surround all four gas giants, but are particularly bright and beautiful around Saturn.

satellite an object that orbits around a larger object. Satellites can be natural, such as moons, or man-made, such as machines that orbit Earth and send back information.

silhouette a dark, shadowed shape seen against a brighter background

solar anything to do with the sun

solar system an area of space containing our sun, the planets and their moons, asteroids, and comets

space everything outside Earth

sun our nearest star. The sun is a huge ball of gas.

telescope an instrument used by astronomers to study objects in space

universe everything that exists

Index